Also available in this series from Quadrille:

the little book of
MIND -FUL- NESS

the little book of
QUIET

the little book of
FRIENDSHIP

the little book of
CONFIDENCE

LOVE

Edited by
Tiddy Rowan

Quadrille
PUBLISHING

Everyone has a love story to tell. And, if not yet, they can be sure that one day they will. It's just a matter of time.

Love is a phenomenon of life. We understand the effects love can have on our bodies; a racing heart, the release of certain hormones, but why we feel it, when we feel it and for whom we feel it, remains a mystery.

But, human nature being what it is, we are impatient, impulsive and impetuous. Our curiosity leads to many a question as to the nature of love in general and in ours particular.

Is it lust, is it love, is it romance or is it friendship? Is it requited or unrequited, is it going to last or be fleeting?

The ancient Greeks had around thirty words to describe love's different meanings for shared emotional feelings alone. They include:

Agape – is the love felt towards humanity, the love of the soul, and a love which gives us a sadness, a longing.

Eros – is the love of passion, of sexual attraction.

Pragma – defines the love which develops over a long period of time, an enduring love, a deep and abiding fondness.

Philia – is a dispassionate love, a virtue, expressing loyalty to both family and the community.

Storge – the natural love felt towards a parent, a child or members of close family.

"Being deeply loved by someone gives you strength, while loving someone deeply gives you courage."

LAO TZU

Love: a big and powerful word to cover the many and varied complexities of human relationships.

We all know what we mean by love – however elusive that meaning is when it comes to describing it to others.

"One word frees us of all the weight and pain of life: That word is love."

SOPHOCLES

" Almost all aspects of life are engineered at the molecular level, and without understanding molecules we can only have a very sketchy understanding of life itself. "

FRANCIS CRICK
What Mad Pursuit

The Science of falling in love

1. Lust – is driven by the sex hormones: testosterone and oestrogen

2. Attraction – at this love-struck phase, scientists think the three neurotransmitters involved are dopamin, noradnenaline and serotonin.

3. Attachment – is the bond that keeps couples together and committed. The two main hormones that can be attributed to this stage are oxytocin and vasopressin. When these are released it helps cement a strong bond between couples.

To know love, you have
to surrender to it.

A commonly shared experience between all of humanity is the experience of falling in love and having a romantic loving relationship. Whether in search of a soulmate to share your life with or experiencing the intensity of a love affair, the emotions experienced are familiar to everyone, irrespective of creed, age, race or culture.

" Sing like no one is listening, love like you've never been hurt, dance like nobody's watching, and live like it's heaven on earth."

MARK TWAIN

Valentine's Day

Valentine's Day is observed every year on 14th February. It is a day to show appreciation for the people you love. It is thought to have derived from the ancient Roman festival, *Lupercalia*, which was a celebration of fertility. It is also thought to have been recast as a Christian celebration of love from the story of St. Valentine, a Roman priest who was martyred on, or around 14th February. The ancient ceremony would have traditionally included boys drawing out the names of girls from a box. Couples would then be paired off until the following year.

"When there is love in a marriage, there is harmony in the home; when there is harmony in the home, there is contentment in the community; when there is contentment in the community, there is prosperity in the nation; when there is prosperity in the nation, there is peace in the world."

CHINESE PROVERB

"If you would be loved, be lovable."

OVID

If only it was that easy to find true love, nurture it and keep it. But it seems there are very few love lessons to learn in life, except for the ones we learn for ourselves.

Nurturing love is key.

Ask yourself some questions; it helps establish how you feel about the relationship.

- Does your love interest make you feel good about yourself?

- Do they accept you for who you are, flaws and all, and make you feel loved just the same?

- Does your loved one support you in the things that are important to you?

- Is your relationship one of give and take?

- Does your girlfriend/boyfriend make an effort to get along with your friends?

- Are they kind to you and take interest in your life and hobbies?

- Are you kind to your love interest?

- When your love interest has let you down, will she/he apologise without being asked?

- Do you miss your love interest when you're apart?

How to make love last?

Poets, writers, artists, lovers and sages continue to grapple with one of life's most elusive questions.

" If love is the answer, could you please rephrase the question?"

LILY TOMLIN

"He is more myself than I am. Whatever our souls are made of, his and mine are the same."

EMILY BRONTË
Wuthering Heights

"Your task is not to seek love, but merely to seek and find all the barriers within yourself that you have built against it."

RUMI

" To love is to suffer. To avoid suffering, one must not love. But, then one suffers from not loving."

WOODY ALLEN

The philosopher Arthur Schopenhauer
looked to aesthetic contemplation
as a temporary escape from the pain
suffered in the craving for love.

A cure for lovesickness

Contemplating art, but finding any form of relaxation or exercise in mindfulness to disengage from frantic thinking, allows the inner expression to surface and guide us.

Music, for many, is considered the purest form of art because it is a timeless, universal language. So it is, perhaps, through music that the meaning of love can be best transmitted.

In search for a distraction to alleviate the frustration in his courtship of Countess Olivia, Duke Orsino says:

"If music be the food of love, play on..."

WILLIAM SHAKESPEARE
Twelfth Night

"I hold it true, whate'er befall;
I feel it, when I sorrow most;
'Tis better to have loved and lost
Than never to have loved at all."

LORD ALFRED TENNYSON

"The one thing we can never get enough of is love. And the one thing we never give enough of is love."

HENRY MILLER
The World of Sex

You can't hurry love

Sometimes persistence pays off. Find a relaxed or even humorous way to be persistent in wooing the one you feel sure is right for you.

" The word love has by no means the same sense for both sexes, and this is one cause of the serious misunderstandings that divide them."

SIMONE DE BEAUVOIR

*"Man's love is of man's life a part;
it is woman's whole existence."*

LORD BYRON

The expression – the feeling of love – is conveyed in the kiss; whether it is passionate, caring, warm or tepid, perfunctory or even side-stepped, will tell us how our lover feels about us.

Which part of loving do you prefer: 'to love' or 'to be loved'? Spending time on finding out this truth helps in understanding the nature of the relationship you are in.

"In a mutual admiration society consisting but of two members; the one whose love is less intense will become president."

ANONYMOUS

Two people discovering they are mutually attracted to each other is a chance encounter, an occurence so magical and rare that it sparks a passionate affair where love is constantly in the air.

"*This, then, is a source of our desire to love each other. Love is born into every human being: it calls back the halves of our original nature together; it tries to make one out of two and heal the wound of human nature.*"

PLATO

" Love alone is capable of uniting living beings in such a way as to complete and fulfill them, for it alone takes them and joins them by what is deepest in themselves."

PIERRE TEILHARD DE CHARDIN

"Love doesn't make the world go round. Love is what makes the ride worthwhile."

FRANKLIN P. JONES

Absinthe makes the heart grow fonder.

" Love consists in this: that two solitudes protect and touch and greet each other."

RAINER MARIA RILKE

Respecting each other's need for independence as well as togetherness is of great importance.

"All mankind loves a lover..."

RALPH WALDO EMERSON

People in love tend to be charming. And everyone around them loves them in turn. Perhaps it is the loving that they are expressing; that is recognised and desired by others.

"*Of all forms of caution, caution in love is perhaps the most fatal to true happiness.*"

BERTRAND RUSSELL
The Conquest of Happiness

Torn between duty and love

"I have found it impossible to carry the heavy burden of responsibility and to discharge my duties as King as I would wish to do without the help and support of the woman I love."

KING EDWARD VIII

Having fallen in love – one of the temptations whilst still in the heady throes of passionate love is to give oneself – one's inner self – completely. But once you have given everything you have nothing left of yourself – and therefore nothing more to give. So be sure to keep a nugget of yourself in a safe place.

" 'Love' is the name for our pursuit of wholeness, for our desire to be complete."

PLATO

" Let me not to the marriage of true minds
Admit impediments. Love is not love
Which alters when it alteration finds,
Or bends with the remover to remove:
O no! it is an ever-fixed mark,
That looks on tempests and
is never shaken."

WILLIAM SHAKESPEARE
Sonnet 116

There is never a right time or a wrong time to tell someone you love them, so follow your heart, go with your instinct and tell your loved one how you feel.

" If you can't laugh together in bed, the chances are you are incompatible, anyway. I'd rather hear a girl laugh well than try to turn me on with long, silent, soulful, secret looks. If you can laugh with a woman, everything else falls into place."

RICHARD FRANCIS BURTON

Laughter is a quick diffuser of rows.

In a relationship – there is never perfect compatibility. There has to be some allowance made for the fact that two people will never truly have the same point of view on everything. Acknowledging that fact might help diffuse arguments. Agreeing to disagree is an option.

"A heart that loves is always young."

GREEK PROVERB

*"The minute I heard my first love story,
I started looking for you, not knowing
how blind that was.
Lovers don't finally meet somewhere.
They're in each other all along."*

RUMI
The Illuminated Rumi

I love you

Tell your partner you love them,
if not every day then often.

Saying 'I love you' reaffirms and
reinforces your love, reassures and
gives your loved one confidence as
it strengthens your commitment to
them and improves the stability of
a relationship.

"Perhaps the feelings that we experience when we are in love represent a normal state. Being in love shows a person who he should be."

ANTON CHEKHOV

Don't be possessive. No one likes someone who is clingy or shows signs of possessiveness. Let him/her enjoy evenings out with their friends or work mates. You don't have to do everything together. While it works for some people – others feel crowded by it. Be perceptive.

Giacomo Casanova (1725 – 1798) was known to be a Venetian smooth-talking charmer who mastered the art of finding, meeting, attracting and seducing beautiful women. Having accomplished his goal, and in fear of forming a relationship that would deny him his freedom, he left the woman and proceeded to find his next conquest. He died alone, even his burial place is unknown. A man who loved – and lost. Or perhaps never loved at all.

Developing a sense of humour and being light-hearted creates a loving disposition. You look better and feel better. And you can't be angry, sad or anxious when you are laughing – or happy.

Three little words with such a powerful meaning...

I love you

The meaning remains no matter how you choose to say it:

I love you
Je t'adore
Ti amo
Seni Seviyorum
Miluji tĕ
S'agapo
Ma armastan sind
Ya tebya liubliu
Ik hou van jou
Miluji te
Jag alskar dig
Te iubesc
Ich liebe dich
Tave myliu
Mahal kita

"Never love anyone who treats you like you're ordinary."

OSCAR WILDE

A note on the art of seduction: it is another curious twist in human behaviour that it is easier to seduce someone if there is not a deeper emotion of like or love in the air but simply a physical attraction.

"To be fond of dancing was a certain step towards falling in love."

JANE AUSTEN

"*My bounty is as boundless as the sea,*
My love as deep; the more I give to thee,
The more I have, for both are infinite."

WILLIAM SHAKESPEARE
Romeo and Juliet

Worth remembering, when in a relationship, that the other person is just as complicated a human being as you are.

What most people want is to be understood and appreciated.

With body, soul and mind entwined, lovers are often consumed by their cohesion. *Egoïsme à deux* – an expression that has come to mean a relationship in which both people are entirely focused on each other.

When difficulties present themselves and – mixed messages ensue, faulty communication, hurt feelings and obscurity lead to unhappiness. It's important to simplify the problem, to untie the knots with empathy.

" It seems essential, in relationships and all tasks, that we concentrate only on what is most significant and important."

SØREN KIERKEGAARD

" To love or have loved, that is enough. Ask nothing further. There is no other pearl to be found in the dark folds of life."

VICTOR HUGO
Les Misérables

Romantic gestures are a good way to show your partner how much you love them. Cook a special, surprise meal for your loved one when it *isn't* a special occasion like a birthday or anniversary and show them how special any day with them is for you.

Compassion is a key ingredient
in giving – and receiving – love.

Be yourself.

"I've always loved you, and when you love someone, you love the whole person, just as he or she is, and not as you would like them to be."

LEO TOLSTOY
Anna Karenina

"There is always some madness in love. But there is also always some reason in madness."

FRIEDRICH NIETZSCHE

And when love grows and flows into a life-long thing it becomes self-perpetuating. Love is in an older couple holding hands as they walk and talk.

"First love is like a revolution; the uniformly regular routine of ordered life is broken down and shattered in one instant; youth mounts the barricade, waves high its bright flag, and whatever awaits it in the future – death or a new life - all alike it goes to meet with ecstatic welcome."

IVAN TURGENEV
Spring Torrents

Don't be stubborn! Give some time to think of the other person's point of view. Sometimes it's good to let go of your opinions.

"Whoever loves, loves at first sight."

WILLIAM SHAKESPEARE
Twelfth Night

"Love is foolish but I still might try it sometime."

ANONYMOUS

" I desire you in friendship, and I will one way or other make you amends."

WILLIAM SHAKESPEARE
The Merry Wives of Windsor

Breathe in slowly, count to two, breathe out slowly counting to five. Do this a few times simply watching your breath, being aware of the gentle in and out that goes on without opinion, without instruction – the beauty of breathing is enough to centre us and calm us.

*"I know of only one duty,
and that is to love."*

ALBERT CAMUS

*"However rare true love may be,
it is less so than true friendship."*

FRANCOIS DE LA ROCHEFOUCAULD

"The world is so empty if one thinks only of mountains, rivers and cities; but to know someone here and there who thinks and feels with us, and who, though distant, is close to us in spirit, this makes the earth for us an inhabited garden."

JOHANN WOLFGANG VON GOETHE
Elective Affinities

In practising love towards humanity;
we need to walk our own paths
advocating a loving heart. Listening
to a friend's concerns, respecting the
welfare of all people and keeping love
alive in our community.

Wedding anniversary gifts by year

- **Year 1:** Paper
- **Year 2:** Cotton
- **Year 3:** Leather
- **Year 4:** Fruit or Flowers
- **Year 5:** Wood
- **Year 6:** Candy or Iron
- **Year 7:** Wool or Copper
- **Year 8:** Bronze or Pottery
- **Year 9:** Pottery
- **Year 10:** Tin
- **Year 11:** Steel
- **Year 12:** Silk or Linen

- **Year 13:** Lace
- **Year 14:** Ivory
- **Year 15:** Crystal
- **Year 20:** China
- **Year 25:** Silver
- **Year 30:** Pearl
- **Year 35:** Coral
- **Year 40:** Ruby
- **Year 45:** Sapphire
- **Year 50:** Gold
- **Year 55:** Emerald
- **Year 60:** Diamond

Love sometimes comes at a cost of what we have to endure or sacrifice – but there's rarely too high a price to pay for true love.

"Women are meant to be loved, not understood."

OSCAR WILDE

"When you realise you want to spend the rest of your life with somebody, you want the rest of your life to start as soon as possible."

When Harry Met Sally
1989

"Friendship is certainly the finest balm for the pangs of disappointed love."

JANE AUSTEN
Northanger Abbey

"Don't forget to love yourself."

SØREN KIERKEGAARD

Learning to love yourself is the key to your own happiness and self-satisfaction. Try these easy activities to help you along:

- Train your mind to think positively.

- Make time each day to focus on yourself and your thoughts.

- Expand your interests and make time for yourself.

- Become willing to surrender. Breathe, relax and let go.

- Forgive yourself. Learn from your mistakes and move forward.

Being in love can indeed blind us to our lover's faults. We see what we want to see – as do they. For better or worse.

"When one loves,
one does not calculate."

THÉRÈSE DE LISIEUX

Philautia: self love

Experts suggest it is important to develop self-respect and self-love in order to truly have love for others – to develop compassion.

To be respected is to respect yourself.

Marcel Proust did not necessarily think that unrequited love was a bad thing because it led to suffering, and in the suffering the soul was laid bare and opened up the way to art; to contemplate art or to create it.

He observes that nothing stokes the would-be lover's love more than telling him or her:

"No, this evening I shan't be free."

"What a profound significance small things assume when the woman we love conceals them from us."

MARCEL PROUST
Remembrance of Things Past

"Love insists the loved loves back."

DANTE ALIGHIERI

Hit by Cupid's arrow.

Cupid in classical mythology is the God of desire, erotic love, attraction and affection. He is the son of Mercury, messenger for the Gods; and Venus, the Goddess of love. His Greek equivalent is Eros. He is usually depicted as a winged infant carrying a bow and arrows whose wounds inspired love or passion.

Cupid is often used as a symbol of St. Valentine's Day.

Love heals

If a problem or anxiety, a disappointment or a loss is experienced – then talking it over with a loved one, or a friend who consoles with a loving heart, is a great healer.

"Those who are seriously concerned with love as the only rational answer to the problem of human existence must, then, arrive at the conclusion that important and radical changes in our social structure are necessary, if love is to become a social and not a highly individualistic, marginal phenomenon."

ERICH FROMM
The Art of Loving

*"I wonder, by my troth,
what thou and I
Did, till we loved?"*

JOHN DONNE
The Good Morrow

"Had I the heavens' embroidered cloths,
Enwrought with golden and silver light,
The blue and the dim and the dark cloths
Of night and light and the half light,
I would spread the cloths under your feet:
But I, being poor, have only my dreams;
I have spread my dreams under your feet;
Tread softly because you tread on my
dreams."

W. B. YEATS
Cloths of Heaven

The Inuit language contains fifty-two names for the word snow because of it's significance to them; there ought to be as many names for love.

> *"The course of true love
> never did run smooth."*

WILLIAM SHAKESPEARE
A Midsummer Night's Dream

Since it is generally agreed that the intense spell of being in love does quieten as the relationship develops; it is the friendship factor that underpins the longevity of the loving relationship.

"If there is such a thing as a good marriage, it is because it resembles friendship rather than love."

MICHEL DE MONTAIGNE

When two people get carried away by their personal points of view; it is already a situation doubled in subjectivity. Diffusing a misunderstanding or problem before it gets blown out of proportion helps towards maintaining harmony.

" The great secret of successful marriage is to treat all disasters as incidents and none of the incidents as disasters."

HAROLD NICOLSON

The fusion in love is the glue
that holds it all together.

"In love, one and one are one."

JEAN-PAUL SARTRE

Love is all things to all people. One of the beauties of it is that it is not prescriptive, but that its meaning is unique to each of us.

"Love is metaphysical gravity."

RICHARD BUCKMINSTER FULLER

When an older couple was asked why they always said 'I love you' to each other at the beginning of each day when one of them went out; they told of how – in case something happened to one of them – they wanted 'I love you' to be the last thing they said to each other.

"The greatest weakness of most humans is their hesitancy to tell others how much they love them while they're still alive."

ORLANDO A. BATTISTA

No matter how many times we love
and maybe lose – it's never too
late to love again.

"If you really love something set it free. If it comes back it's yours, if not it wasn't meant to be."

ANONYMOUS

We measure our success in different ways – but it is not all about money, position, power or job promotions. Love is a factor.

Better love than money
if a choice had to be made.

Of course we always want the weather to be nice; but we know – realistically – that once in a while there will be rain and storms. The cycle of love is much the same.

"*Oh, life is a glorious cycle of song,
A medley of extemporanea; And love
is a thing that can never go wrong;
And I am Marie of Roumania.*"

DOROTHY PARKER

Enough Rope

The Atlantic puffin mates for life. Once they reach breeding age; between three and six years old, this clown among seabirds will seek a partner with whom they will mate with for the rest of their life. During courtship the mated pair will touch or clasp their partner's beak, which is known as billing. This behaviour strengthens and reaffirms the pair's bond each year as they embark on rearing their young for another season. The pair will happily share the same burrow and egg-incubating and parenting duties.

"It is as absurd to say that a man can't love one woman all the time as it is to say that a violinist needs several violins to play the same piece of music."

HONORÉ DE BALZAC

Just as much as it's impossible for a
pretence of loving not to show, so too
is it impossible not to see love where
it exists. Truth in love is potent.

"No disguise can long conceal love where it exists, or long feign it where it is lacking."

FRANÇOIS DE LA ROCHEFOUCAULD

When a relationship develops and matures; close proximity and the habit of the familiar can lead to dullness. Mindfulness is a good way of keeping things fresh; making sure everyone has enough space – mental as well as physical.

*" The more one judges,
the less one loves."*

HONORÉ DE BALZAC

Make love not war.

" To love a thing is wanting it to live."

CONFUCIUS

Don't let words and misunderstandings get in the way of feelings.

" To love you must be willing to let go,
to let go you must be willing to love."

ANONYMOUS

It's not always the big shows
of love that count in life.

" Do not think that love in order to be genuine has to be extraordinary. What we need is to love without getting tired. Be faithful in small things because it is in them that your strength lies."

MOTHER TERESA

Love becomes part of us,
as we become part of love.

"It isn't possible to love and part. You will wish that it was. You can transmute love, ignore it, muddle it, but you can never pull it out of you. I know by experience that the poets are right: love is eternal."

E. M. FORSTER
A Room with a View

The difference between cut flowers and flowers for life is that for the latter there is the pleasure of finding the right conditions, the right soil and the right tending, whereas the cut ones are but a brief encounter.

You can't be everyone's cup of tea.

There should be no room for the ego to control others in love.

"Age does not protect you from love. But love, to some extent, protects you from age."

JEANNE MOREAU

Travel light: let go of hatred, envy, resentment and blame.

*"I have decided to stick to love...
Hate is too great a burden to bear."*

MARTIN LUTHER KING JR
A Testament of Hope

Really – when you think about it –
life is too short. Make love last long.

"Life is short, break the rules.
Forgive quickly, kiss slowly.
Love truly. Laugh uncontrollably
And never regret anything
That made you smile."

MARK TWAIN

Fear is a great impediment. The more we conquer fear within, the more we open up to the possibilities of love in our life.

"But the strong base and building of my love is as the very centre of the earth, drawing all things to it."

WILLIAM SHAKESPEARE

Troilus and Cressida

Making people feel good about themselves is a key element in compassion and mindful loving.

"He stepped down, trying not to look long at her, as if she were the sun, yet he saw her, like the sun, even without looking."

LEO TOLSTOY
Anna Karenina

"He looked at her the way all women want to be looked at by a man."

F. SCOTT FITZGERALD
The Great Gatsby

Love is not only to do with love
directed towards one person. It
is an all-enveloping energy. It is
unmissable. It shines. Practice love
whenever and wherever you can.

If you have to question how you feel, if you are not sure... then it's probably not love. Not until you recognise it.

*"On me your voice falls,
as they say love should be
– like an enormous 'yes'."*

PHILIP LARKIN
For Sidney Bechet

*"Love conquers all things:
let us too give in to love."*

VIRGIL
Eclogues

People often equate that sense of longing with the quest to find a soulmate as much as a bed-mate.

It is perhaps the first thrill of being in love – thinking for a moment that we have gone beyond earthly biologics and soared into the heights of nothing other than supreme romantic destiny.

"The goal in marriage is not to think alike, but to think together."

ROBERT C. DODDS

"To laugh often and love much... to appreciate beauty, to find the best in others, to give one's self... this is to have succeeded."

RALPH WALDO EMERSON

"Love is a canvas furnished by nature and embroidered by imagination."

VOLTAIRE

Be loved for you. Don't change for anyone. True love doesn't require you to be someone else.

"If you press me to say why I loved him, I can say no more than because he was he, and I was I."

MICHEL DE MONTAIGNE

When the first sparks of a romance die down and your love becomes a constant; it is the little gestures that count as much as the big ones.

Romantic love in the western world is rooted in the classical Christian vision of the human condition, which in turn is based on Aristotelean philosophy and reflected in the works of Shakespeare, Dante and the French Romantic poets. In the east; similar values expressed in literature, namely compassion and a tender love towards our fellow human beings, were rooted in the teachings of Buddha.

In fact; it's safe to say that all religions in the world advocate love as part of their canon.

True love is not fleeting.

"He who binds to himself a joy
Doth the winged life destroy.
But he who kisses a joy as it flies
Lives in eternity's sunrise."

WILLIAM BLAKE

Regain your spark

Think back to what attracted
your loved one to you...

Keep that in mind when you want
to spark things up between you.

"Passion is the quickest to develop, and the quickest to fade. Intimacy develops more slowly, and commitment more gradually still."

ROBERT STERNBERG

One conundrum in the puzzle of love is how to arrive at a mutual understanding of what two people want from a relationship and whether they are both travelling towards the same point. Therein lies part of the mystery. But where there is complete lack of clarity there is agony. When there is harmony and clarity; there is ecstasy. A degree of transparency and honesty is essential.

"*When we hug, our hearts connect and we know that we are not separate beings. Hugging with mindfulness and concentration can bring reconciliation, healing, understanding and much happiness.*"

THICH NHAT HANH

When in love, songs, films and books can take on different meanings. Suddenly everything is related and every word we read and hear, every lyric sung has a greater significance. It feels like fate, a happy coincidence that somehow your emotions were captured.

"Always toward absent lovers love's tide stronger flows."

SEXTUS PROPERTIUS
Elegies

The three Cs to keep in mind:

Confidence – Courage – Compassion

"Friendship with oneself is all-important because without it one cannot be friends with anyone else in the world."

ELEANOR ROOSEVELT

*"Love is an irresistible desire
to be irresistibly desired."*

ROBERT FROST

Although falling in love is one of life's greatest pleasures and passions – we need to protect and nurture all the many varieties of love in our lives; the love of our families, our friends, to humanity and all the many things that we hold important in the world.

"Let us always meet each other with a smile, for the smile is the beginning of love."

MOTHER TERESA

BIBLIOGRAPHY

Books mentioned in *The Little Book of Love*

Austen, Jane. *Northanger Abbey* (1817)

Bernières, Louis de. *Captain Corelli's Mandolin* (Vintage, 1998)

Brontë, Emily. *Wuthering Heights* (1874)

Crick, Francis. *What Mad Pursuit: A Personal View of Scientific Discovery* (Basic Books, 1990)

Donne, John. *The Good Morrow* (1633)

Fitzgerald, F. Scott. *The Great Gatsby* (Charles Scribner's Sons, 1925)

Forster, E. M. *A Room with a View* (Edward Arnold Publishers, 1908)

Fromm, Erich. *The Art of Loving* (Harper & Row, 1956)

Goethe, Johann Wolfgang von. *Elective Affinities* (1809)

Hugo, Victor. *Les Misérables* (1862)

King, Martin Luther, Jr. *A Testament of Hope: The Essential Writings and Speeches* (Harper Collins, 1991)

Larkin, Philip. *For Sidney Bechet* (1954)

Miller, Henry. *The World of Sex* (1940)

Rumi. *The Illuminated Rumi* (1997)

Russell, Bertrand. *The Conquest of Happiness* (1958)

Parker, Dorothy. *Enough Rope* (1926)

Properius, Sextus. *Elegies* (29 BCE)

Proust, Marcel. *Remembrance of Things Past* (1923)

Shakespeare, William. *A Midsummer Night's Dream* (1596)

Shakespeare, William. *Romeo and Juliet* (1595)

Shakespeare, William. *Sonnet 116* (1609)

Shakespeare, William. *The Merry Wives of Windsor* (1602)

Shakespeare, William. *Troilus and Cressida* (1602)

Shakespeare, William. *Twelfth Night* (1623)

Tennyson, Alfred. *In Memoriam* (1901)

Tolstoy, Leo. *Anna Karenina* (Thomas Y. Crowell & Co., 1887)

Turgenev, Ivan. *Spring Torrents* (Eyre Methuen Ltd, 1972)

Virgil, *Eclogues*. no. 10,177 (37 BC)

Yeats, W. B. *Cloth of Heaven* (1899)

Further reading

Rowan, Tiddy. *The Little Book of Mindfulness* (Quadrille, 2013)

Films

When Harry Met Sally, directed by Rob Reiner (Castle Rock Entertainment, 1989)

Websites

Fisher, Maryanne, *Psychology Today*, "The Science Behind Falling in Love," (2013). Available at: www.psychologytoday.com/blog/loves-evolver/201302/the-science-behind-falling-in-love

QUOTES ARE TAKEN FROM:

Albert Camus was a French-Algerian author and philosopher. He was awarded the Nobel Prize for Literature in 1957.

Alfred Tennyson is one of Britain's most popular poets.

Anton Chekhov was a Russian physician and author.

Bertrand Russell was a British philosopher, mathematician, historian and political activist; and a champion of anti-imperialism.

Confucius was an influential Chinese teacher, philosopher and political.

Dante Alighieri was an Italian poet of the Middle Ages, well known for his work *Divine Comedy*.

Dorothy Parker was an American writer and poet and founding member of the Algonquin Round Table.

E. M. Forster (Edward Morgan Forster) was an English novelist well remembered for his titles *Howards End* and *A Room with a View*.

Eleanor Roosevelt was an American politician and wife of President Franklin Roosevelt.

Emily Brontë wrote only one book – *Wuthering Heights* – but it is considered a seminal landmark in Gothic fiction.

Erich Fromm was a German social psychologist, psychoanalyst and humanistic philosopher.

Francis Crick was one of Britain's greatest scientists and best known for his work, which led to the identification of the structure of DNA in 1953.

Francis Scott Fitzgerald was an American author who is well known for his novels *The Great Gatsby* and *The Beautiful and Damned*.

François de La Rochefoucauld (Prince de Marcillac) was a noted French author of maxims and memoirs.

Franklin P. Jones was an American reporter and humourist.

Friedrich Nietzsche was a German philosopher and poet.

Johann Wolfgang von Goethe was a German writer and statesman and is considered the greatest German literary figure.

Harold Nicolson was an English diplomat, author and politician.

Henry Miller was an American writer. His most characteristic works include *Tropic of Cancer* and *Black Spring*.

Honoré de Balzac was a French novelist and playwright.

Ivan Turgenev was a Russian novelist best known for his novel *Fathers and Sons*.

Jean Liedloff was an American author of *The Continuum Concept*.

Jean-Paul Sartre was a French philosopher, novelist and literary critic. He was a leading figures in the philosophy of existentialism.

Jeanne Moreau was a French actress, singer and director.

John Donne was an English poet and cleric in the Church of England.

King Edward VIII was the eldest son of Kind George V and was crowned king in January 1936 after his father's death. He then abdicated in December 1936 to marry divorcée Wallis Simpson.

Lao Tzu was a philosopher and poet of ancient China, best known for his work *Tao Te Ching*.

Leo Tolstoy was a Russian writer, philosopher and political thinker who penned *War and Peace* and *Anna Karenina*.

Lily Tomlin was an American actress and comedian.

Lord Byron was a British poet and leading figure in the Romantic movement.

Louis de Bernières is a British novelist.

Marcel Proust was a French novelist best known for his monumental novel *Remeberance of Thing Past*.

Mark Twain was an American author and humourist. He was the author of *The Adventures of Tom Sawyer* and *Huckleberry Finn*.

Martin Luther King Jr was an American pastor, activist and leader who led the Civil Rights Movement in the United States from the mid-1950s until his death in 1968.

Michel de Montaigne was an influential writer during the French Renaissance.

Mother Teresa was the founder of the order of the Missionaries of Charity, a Roman Catholic congregation of women.

Orlando A. Battista was a Canadian-American chemist and author.

Oscar Wilde was an Irish writer, playwright and poet. He is best known for his book *The Picture of Dorian Gray*.

Philip Larkin was an English poet and novelist. His first book of poetry, *The North Ship*, was published in 1945.

Pierre Teilhard de Chardin was a French philosopher and Jesuit priest.

Plato was a philosopher as well a mathematician in Classical Greece.

Richard Buckminster Fuller was an American neo-futuristic architect, author, designer and inventor.

Rainer Maria Rilke was an Austrian poet and philosopher.

Ralph Waldo Emerson was an American essayist and poet who led the Transcendentalist movement in the mid 19th century.

Richard Francis Burton was an English geographer and explorer.

Robert C. Dodds was a former official of the National Council of Churches and a psychologist.

Robert Frost was an American poet. He received four Pulitzer Prizes for his poetry throughout his lifetime and he was awarded the Congressional Gold Medal in 1960 for his poetic works.

Robert Sternberg is an American psychologist.

Rumi was a 13th-century Persian poet, theologian and Sufi mystic.

Sextus Propertius was a Latin elegiac poet of the Augustan age.

Simone de Beauvoir was a French writer and an existentialist philosopher. She is best known for her novels *The Mandarins* and *She Came to Stay*.

Sophocles was the second of the three ancient Greek writers of tragedy. He was best known for what he wrote about Oedipus.

Soren Kierkegaard was a Danish philosopher and theologian. He is widely considered to be the first existentialist philosopher.

Thérèse de Lisieux was a French Discalced Carmelite nun.

Thich Nhat Hanh is a Vietnamese Zen Buddist monk, author and peace activist.

Victor Hugo was a French poet and dramatist of the Romantic movement. His works include *Les Misérables* and *Notre-Dame de Paris*.

Virgil (Publius Vergilius Maro) was an ancient Roman poet of the Augustus period.

Voltaire (François-Marie Arouet) was a French Enlightenment writer, historain and philosopher.

W. B. Yeats (William Butler Yeats) was an Irish poet and leading literary figure of the 20th century.

William Blake was an English painter and poet. He is considered a seminal figure of poetry and visual arts of the Romantic Age.

William Shakespeare was an English poet, actor and playwright. His works include *Hamlet*, *Macbeth* and *King Lear*.

Woody Allen (Heywood Allen) is an American actor, director and comedian.

PAGE REFERENCES

Page 12: Crick, Francis, *What Mad Pursuit* (Basic Books, 1990)

Page 26: Brontë, Emily, Wuthering Heights (1847)

Page 32: Shakespeare, William, *Twelfth Night* (1623)

Page 34: Miller, Henry. *The World of Sex* (1940)

Page 42: Plato: from a speech given by aristophanes included in the symposium.

Page 50: Russell, Bertrand, *The Conquest of Happiness* (1958)

Page 51: Edward VIII: from his annoucement of his abdication of the throne speech (1936)

Page 53: Plato: from a speech given by aristophanes included in the symposium.

Page 54: Shakespeare, William, *Sonnet 116* (1609)

Page 60: Rumi, *The Illuminated Rumi* (1997)

Page 71: Shakespeare, William, *Romeo and Juilet* (1595)

Page 77: Hugo, Victor, *Les Misérables* (1862)

Page 81: Tolstoy, Leo, *Anna Karenina* (Thomas Y. Crowell & Co., 1887)

Page 84: Turgenev, Ivan, *Spring Torrents* (Eyre Methuen Ltd, 1972)

Page 86: Shakespeare, William, *Twelfth Night* (1623)

Page 88: Shakespeare, William, *The Merry Wives of Windsor* (1602)

Page 92: Goethe, JohannWolfgang von, *Elective Affinities* (1809)

Page 98: *When Harry Met Sally* (Castle Rock Entertainment, 1989)

Page 99: Austen, Jane, *Northanger Abbey* (1817)

Page 107: Proust, Marcel, *Remembrance of Things Past*, "The Captive" (1923)

Page 111: Fromm, Erich, *The Art of Loving* (Harper & Row, 1956)

Page 112: Donne, John, *The Good Morrow* (1633)

Page 113: Yeats, W. B, *Cloth of Heaven* (1899)

Page 115: Shakespeare, William, *A Midsummer Night's Dream* (1596)

Page 131: Parker, Dorothy**,** *Enough Rope* (1929)

Page 145: Forster, E. M, *A Room with a View* (Edward Arnold Publishers, 1908)

Page 151: King, Martin Luther, Jr, *A Testament of Hope: The Essential Writings and Speeches,* (Harper Collins, 1991)

Page 155: Shakespeare, William, *Troilus and Cressida* (1602)

Page 157: Tolstoy, Leo, *Anna Karenina* (Thomas Y. Crowell & Co., 1887)

Page 158: Fitzgerald, F. Scott, *The Great Gatsby* (Charles Scribner's Sons, 1925)

Page 161: Larkin, Philip, *For Sidney Bechet* (1954)

Page 162: Virgil, *Eclogues*, no. 10,177 (37 BC)

Page 178: Propertius, Sextus, *The Elegies* (29 BCE)

Editorial director Anne Furniss
Creative director Helen Lewis
Editorial assistant Harriet Butt
Designer Emily Lapworth
Production director Vincent Smith
Production controller Emily Noto

First published in 2015 by
Quadrille Publishing Ltd
Pentagon House
52-54 Southwark Street
London SE1 1UN
www.quadrille.co.uk

Quadrille is an imprint of Hardie Grant.
www.hardiegrant.com.au

British Library Cataloguing-in-Publication Data
A catalogue record for this book is available from the British Library.

ISBN: 978 1 84949 561 5

Printed in China